Take a trip to

HAWAII

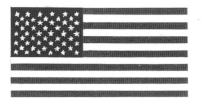

Keith Lye

Franklin Watts

London   New York   Sydney   Toronto

Facts about Hawaii

Area:
16,759 sq. km.
(6,471 sq. miles)

Population:
1,054,000

Capital:
Honolulu

Largest cities:
Honolulu (365,000)
Pearl City (43,000)
Kailua (35,800)
Hilo (35,300)

Official language:
English

Religion:
Christianity

Main products:
Manufactures (especially sugar, canned fruit, fruit juices and other food), farm products

Currency:
US dollar

Franklin Watts
12a Golden Square
London W1

Franklin Watts Inc.
387 Park Avenue South
New York, N.Y. 10016

ISBN: UK Edition 0 86313 647 8
ISBN: US Edition 0 531 10466 4
Library of Congress Catalog Card No:
87-51070

Typeset by Ace Filmsetting Ltd.,
Frome, Somerset
Printed in Hong Kong

© Franklin Watts Limited 1988

Maps: Simon Roulstone
Design: Edward Kinsey
Stamps: Harry Allen International
Philatelic Distributors
Photographs: Barnaby's Picture
Library, 14, 19, 25, 27, 28, 29;
Hawaii Visitor's Bureau, 4, 5, 16, 20,
21, 24, 26; Tony Stone Associates, 9,
10, 11, 17, 18, 22, 23, 30, 31; Zefa, 6,
7, 8, 15

Front Cover: Zefa
Back Cover: Tony Stone Associates

Hawaii is one of the 50 states which make up the United States. It contains eight large islands and 124 small ones in the North Pacific Ocean. The combined area of the 124 small islands is only 8 sq km (3 sq miles). Hawaii's nickname is Aloha, a Hawaiian word for "love".

The largest island is also called Hawaii, or the "Big Island". It covers 10,458 sq km (4,038 sq miles). It has magnificent scenery and some huge volcanoes. One of them, the snow-capped Mauna Kea, is the state's highest mountain. It rises 4,205 m (13,796 ft) above sea level.

The islands of Hawaii were formed by volcanoes which rise from the sea bed. Two volcanoes, Mauna Loa and Kilauea, are in the Hawaii Volcanoes National Park on Big Island. These volcanoes sometimes hurl lava (molten rock) into the air. Streams of lava often flow downhill.

Maui, the second biggest island, covers 1,888 sq km (729 sq miles). It has a National Park, which contains the crater of Haleakala, a dormant (sleeping) volcano. This volcano has not erupted for more than a hundred years.

Oahu is the third largest island. It covers 1,575 sq km (608 sq miles). Oahu is important because it is the home for four out of every five people who live in the state. Honolulu, on Oahu, is the state's capital and largest city.

Hawaii has a pleasant climate throughout the year. It attracts many tourists from North America and other parts of the world. Honolulu is a major tourist city. It contains the famous resort, Waikiki Beach.

Kauai is the state's fourth largest island. It has an area of 1,432 sq km (553 sq miles). Like the other islands, it is made of volcanic rock. Fast flowing streams have worn out deep canyons.

Kauai is a lush, green island. In the middle is Mount Waialeale, which is one of the world's wettest places. Its average yearly rainfall is 1,234 cm (486 inches). Most mountain regions in Hawaii get plenty of rain, but the lowlands are drier.

Molokai, the fifth largest island, covers 676 sq km (261 sq miles). Its north coast is so rugged that the only way to reach it is by boat. The other three large islands in Hawaii are, in order of size, Lanai, Niihau and the uninhabited Kahoolawe.

The picture shows some of the money and stamps used in Hawaii. The main unit of currency is the US dollar. It is divided into 100 cents.

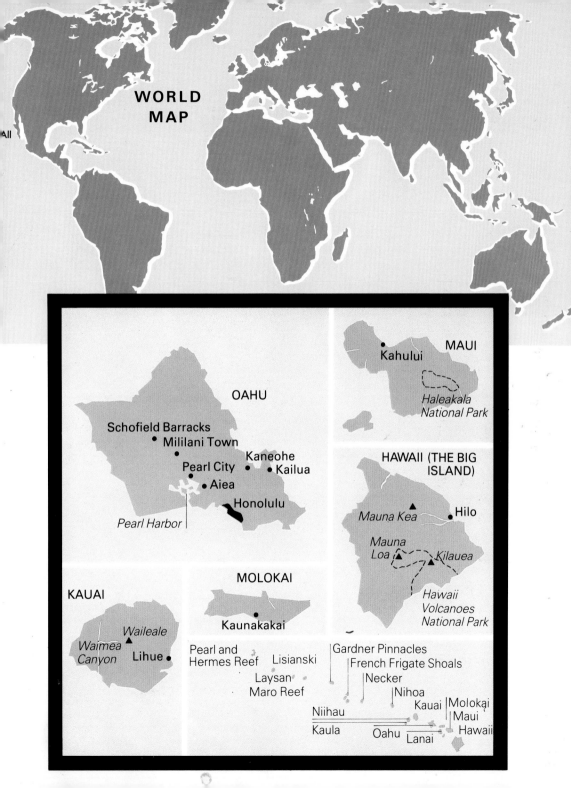

WORLD MAP

OAHU

Schofield Barracks
Mililani Town
Kaneohe
Pearl City
Kailua
Aiea
Honolulu
Pearl Harbor

MAUI

Kahului

Haleakala
National Park

HAWAII (THE BIG
ISLAND)

Mauna Kea
Hilo
Mauna
Loa
Kilauea

Hawaii
Volcanoes
National Park

KAUAI

Waileale
Waimea
Canyon
Lihue

MOLOKAI

Kaunakakai

Pearl and
Hermes Reef
Lisianski
Laysan
Maro Reef

Gardner Pinnacles
French Frigate Shoals
Necker
Nihoa
Kauai
Molokai
Maui
Hawaii
Niihau
Kaula
Oahu
Lanai

The first people to live in Hawaii
were Polynesians. These people are
related to the Maoris of New Zealand
and to many other Pacific islanders.
Nearly everyone in Hawaii speaks
English. Some Polynesians also speak
their ancient language.

About a fifth of Hawaiians are
Polynesians. Some wear traditional
clothes on special occasions. People
of European and Japanese descent
make up large groups. There are also
people of Filipino, Chinese, Korean
and Samoan origin.

The first European to see Hawaii was the British explorer Captain James Cook in 1778. He was killed on the Big Island in a battle with the Hawaiians in January 1779. A memorial marks the spot.

When Cook arrived, each of the large islands had its own ruler. But between 1790 and 1819, King Kamehameha I united the islands and founded the Kingdom of Hawaii. This statue of the king is in Honolulu.

American missionaries settled in Hawaii in 1820. They were Protestants. Roman Catholics first arrived in 1827. Many beautiful churches were built, including the Painted Church on the Big Island.

One famous missionary, a Belgian Roman Catholic priest named Father Damien, went to Molokai Island in 1873 and built a church there. He helped people suffering from Hansen's disease (or leprosy).

Hawaii became a republic in 1894. The United States took over the government of the islands in 1898 and, in 1959, Hawaii became the 50th state of the United States. Hawaii's laws are made in the State Capitol, in Honolulu.

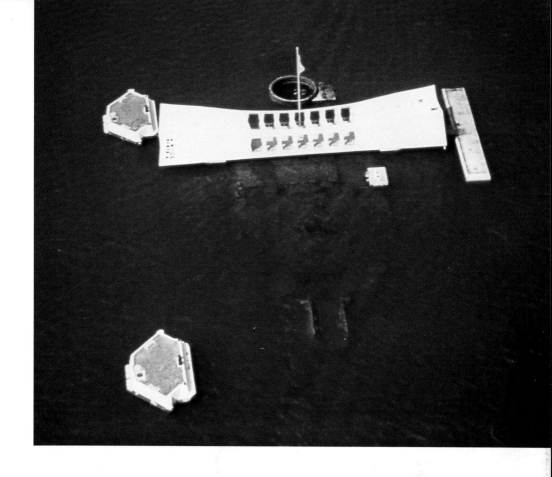

Japan attacked the American fleet in Pearl Harbor on Oahu on December 7 1941. This led the United States to enter World War II. The battleship *Arizona* was sunk and a memorial now stands above the ship. Oahu remains an important military base.

Hawaii is a prosperous state. Farming accounts for a third of the value of goods produced there. Manufacturing accounts for most of the rest. Sugar cane is the leading crop. It grows on about three-quarters of the state's cropland.

Pineapples are Hawaii's second most valuable crop. Food processing is the main manufacturing industry. Canned fruit and fruit juices are leading items. Farmers also produce beef, dairy products and many kinds of fruits and vegetables.

Fresh fruit and vegetables are
popular in Hawaii. There are many
kinds of restaurants, serving North
American, Asian and European foods.
Luaus (feasts) attract many tourists.
At luaus, pigs are roasted in pits.

24

Fish is another popular food. The leading fish caught in the sea is a type of tuna called skipjack. Fish are also reared in ponds and tanks on fish farms. Deep sea and river fishing are leading sports.

On special occasions, Hawaiians wear wreaths of flowers around their necks. These wreaths are called leis. These beautiful garlands are also made for export. Huge displays of leis are on display on May 1, Lei Day.

Ships transport food and other products between the islands of Hawaii. But passengers who are in a hurry use the airlines. Honolulu has an international airport. This seaport is on Kauai Island.

Many young people travel around on bicycles. Education for children between 6 and 18 years of age is free and compulsory. The first schools were founded by the early Christian missionaries.

Most Hawaiians are Christians
and Christmas is a major family
holiday. Christmas trees are imported
from North America, though tropical
Hawaii grows Norfolk pines, which
make fine Christmas trees.

Dancing, called hula, is a leading art form in Hawaii. The graceful dancers learn to sway their hips and wave their arms. The picture shows a dance lesson for people of all ages at Waikiki Beach, Oahu.

Visitors to Waikiki Beach are entertained by hula dancers and musicians. Hawaii is a remote region. In 1955 only about 110,000 tourists went there. Today about five million tourists arrive each year.

Index

DATE DUE

NOV 23 2009		
JUN 04 2011		
AUG 14 2012		

GAYLORD   #3523PI   Printed in USA